BOOK ANALYSIS

Written by Dominique Coutant-Defer and Alexandre Randal

Translated by Ciaran Traynor

AF131421

The Officers' Ward
BY MARC DUGAIN

MARC DUGAIN

FRENCH AUTHOR, THEATRE DIRECTOR AND FILMMAKER

- **Born in Senegal in 1957.**
- **Notable works**:
  - *The Officers' Ward* (1998), novel
  - *Une exécution ordinaire* ("An Ordinary Execution", 2000), novel
  - *La Bonté des femmes* ("The Kindness of Women", 2011), film

Marc Dugain was born in Senegal to French parents. Before becoming a writer, worked in political science, finance and aeronautics. He then turned to writing and began to publish books (*The Officers' Ward*; *La Malédiction d'Edgar* ["The Curse of Edgar"], 2005; *Une exécution ordinaire*) which featured various characters – officers, businessmen, directors – in critical situations (war, power, espionage). He is also the author of a comic book, has written several collections of short stories, and directed a play. The success of *The Officers' Ward* led him to adapt it for the cinema in 2001. He also directed the adaptation of *Une exécution ordinaire* in 2010.

THE OFFICERS' WARD

WHEN WAR DESTROYS EVERY LAST SHRED OF HUMANITY

- **Genre**: novel
- **Reference edition**: Dugain, M. (2001) *The Officers' Ward*. Trans. Curtis, H. London: Phoenix
- **1st edition**: 1999 (Original work published in France in 1998)
- **Themes**: First World War, "gueules cassées", stares, hope, suffering, trauma

The Officers' Ward was published in 1998 and was extremely successful. The author was inspired to write this short, simple and concise novel by his childhood spent with his grandfather in his "chateau de Gueules cassées" ("Castle of Broken Faces"). It is written from the point of view of Adrien Fournier, a young French officer who suffers a serious facial injury at the start of the offensive in 1914. The novel is about his experience of the war.

Adrien spends the war at the Val-de-Grâce hospital in Paris, where he goes through a number of operations. However, none of them can restore his face to the way it used to look. He makes friends with two other injured officers who are also in the hospital. Once he goes back to civilian life, he has to endure the stares of others, gets married and manages to lead a normal life.

SUMMARY

The novel has a linear plot and follows a chronological order: leaving for war, injury, lengthy hospitalisation, recovery and, finally, return to civilian life.

WAR WOUNDS

In 1914, Adrien Fournier is conscripted into the army. He has to leave Périgord, the region where he was born, to go to Paris to take a train to the front. At the station, he meets a young woman called Clémence, who is completely distraught because her fiancé has just gone off to war. Adrien decides to take the train the next day and spends the night with the young woman in the apartment he is renting in Paris. He falls in love with her and leaves her a letter, hoping he will see her again.

He arrives at his quarters in Meuse, northeast France, and witnesses the death of one of his men on the very first day. He is stunned. Some time later, when he is on a reconnaissance mission, he falls into an ambush. A detonation rings out nearby, blowing away half of his face. He explains that he"felt as if an axe had embedded itself just under my nose. Then the light went out".

He is unconscious for several days, before waking up in a countryside hospital. He can neither talk nor eat, is in great deal of pain and has lost his sense of smell. He is transferred to the Val-de-Grâce military hospital in Paris. The war has "well and truly started". He is put in a mirrorless room reserved for officers. He undergoes his first operation and is finally able to get up.

The rooms reserved for ordinary soldiers are full and two new officers, Penanster and Weil, are put beside him. They play cards together to kill time. Over the next 13 months, a string of injured soldiers come to the hospital and either die, or leave once they have been "vaguely patched up". However, some of them commit suicide, unable to cope with their despair. Adrien and his friends decide to do everything they can to stop further suicide attempts, which are becoming more and more common at the hospital.

He writes to his parents and plays down his injuries, saying that "I wanted them to ignore me, not even think about me, much less worry about me." When his best friend, Alain Bonnard, comes to visit him, Adrien sees the horror in his eyes. As a result, he refuses to see his cousins and no longer wants to leave the hospital, feeling "more comfortable here, among my comrades". Later on, he finds out the awful news that Alain has died. Even though he was declared unfit for military service, his friend had insisted on being sent to the front.

Each night, the young man dreams of Clémence. However, she sends him a letter to tell him that she does not want to see him again. Even though he is disappointed, he still hopes that he will have the chance to "see time blur her figure and make inroads into her beauty". He explains that he will never get old, "not with my mutilated face". Moreover, he begins to wish for the monotony of a monk's life, "with an extra dose of suffering, and without the spiritual enlightenment.

After this, Adrien is given his first skin graft, which is unsuccessful, but the doctor remains confident. Some time later, he is given a set of false teeth, which finally allow him to form words again. Intense bonds now form between the three permanent occupants of the room. They make the unspoken decision not to think about their situation too much or consider themselves martyrs.

Later on, Weil discovers that a nurse from the front line called Marguerite, who has also suffered a facial wound ("she was like a bed of roses from which the flowers in the middle had been uprooted), is now in the room beside them. She has lost her hearing and has to communicate with the three men through gestures. The four get along well.

On 14 July, they decide to leave the hospital. However, Adrien begins to panic once he is outside and cannot meet the eyes of passersby. The three men try again to interact with women, this time in a brothel, far from public attention. However, Adrien is extremely unsettled by the experience.

In February 1917, he reluctantly agrees to a visit from his sister, who looks him in the eyes without flinching, and then his mother, who is simply happy that her son is alive.

A few months later, the wounded begin to regain hope after they find out that the Americans have joined the war, which will perhaps make the war end sooner. Adrien and his two friends then consider leaving for Africa, because "in Africa a disfigured warrior was treated like a lord". The armistice is finally signed on 11 November 1918: "it was a also huge relief – it had not all been for nothing", Adrien explains.

RETURN TO CIVILIAN LIFE

The young man leaves the hospital in April 1919. He now has to get used to uncomfortable and sympathetic looks. "Despite 16 operations, my face still did not look human", he notes. He insists on going back to his job as a commercial engineer, even though his old boss offers him a job out of the public eye. He slowly begins to accept the way he is and refuses to get plastic surgery.

Some time later, he is invited by Georges Clémenceau (Prime Minister of France during the First World War, 1841-1929) to receive the Legion of Honour and witness the signing of the Treaty of Versailles. He is happy that his sacrifice has been recognised, but even happier to see Penanster and Weil again. Penanster goes back to Brittany, while Weil works in the airport in Bourget. Together, they create an association of "gueules cassés" (broken faces), which Marguerite, who has gone back to being a nurse, also joins. However, she is still single, because "a disfigured woman is something the world cannot deal with".

Adrien also sees Clémence again. It turns out that her fiancé died in the war. She agrees to be friends with him, but the two drift apart when Adrien gets married in 1924 and becomes a father in 1926. They do not see each other again until 1928, when Clémence has also got married. However, she admits that if they had met up again earlier, she might have married him, which throws Adrien a little off balance.

In 1940, Adrien goes to stay with Penanster, unable to bear the presence of the Germans in Paris. They also take in Weil, who is in danger because he is Jewish. A few years later, Penanster is killed in a fall. His funeral is in the Saint-Louis-des-Invalides Church in Paris. The funeral is attended by Marguerite and many soldiers who have been injured in the Second World War (1939-1945), who are intimidated by their comrades who fought in the First World War. Adrien and Weil set themselves a new mission to "teach them how to enjoy life" so they can overcome their trauma, just like they managed to overcome their own.

CHARACTER STUDY

24-year-old Adrien is the narrator of the novel. He graduated as an Engineer in Applied Arts and becomes a lieutenant in the army. Clémence tells him he has a "perfect face". He spent a happy childhood in Périgord and often reminisces about this time in his life. He works in Paris, where he rents an apartment.

Nothing prepares him for war. He enjoys life and feels close to nature, who upholds "pagan values, particularly the gathering of wild mushrooms when the chestnut trees were in blossom". He thinks God is "a little fellow without a tail". He seems to drift through his conscription in a state of obliviousness, which is reinforced by the fact that he meets Clémence at the same time. His arrival at the front reminds him of "the first day at school". It is only after witnessing the death of a man in his unit that he realises that "the first day of school was over".

Throughout the story, he maintains a degree of detachment from events, simply regretting the irony of being "defeated without even fighting" and the absurdity of his injury. Since he is wounded in the first days of the war, he has no epic war stories to tell later.

His hospitalisation changes the way he thinks. It also helps him to help others and, paradoxically, since he can no longer talk, to communicate better. With a great deal of courage, he manages to overcome his pain and once again face the eyes of society.

HENRI DE PENANSTER

Henri de Penanster is a Breton aristocrat and a cavalry captain who was injured in the Forest of Argonne. He is extremely religious and spends some of his time in hospital carving a wooden sculpture of the Virgin Mary. His friends are impressed by him.

PIERRE WEIL

Pierre Weil is a Jewish pilot who is seriously burned when his plane is attacked by the enemy. He comes to the hospital at the same time as Penanster. He is a more extroverted than his friend, and quickly proves to be a lively man and a bon vivant who often amuses the others with his unusual sense of humour: he says he does not want "a little nose", he wants "a proper Jewish nose".

ALAIN BONNARD

Alain Bonnard is the narrator's best friend. He is also an engineer. He was born with a small right hand and wishes he could have signed up to join the army. He makes up for his disability with his intelligence and admires Adrien, who knows that "I represented a degree of physical accomplishment which he would gladly have traded with me, even if it also meant acquiring my weaker brain". The two young men are very close, in spite of the fact that they seem to be the polar opposites of one another.

CLÉMENCE

Clémence is the fiancée of a pianist who dies at the front. She is also a musician and a regular of the artistic haunts of the capital. She hates the countryside, unlike Adrien, a man of the earth who appreciates the simple pleasures in life. Adrien falls in love with her – something that he says he has never experienced – from the very first time they meet.

After at first rejecting Adrien, she ends up agreeing to be friends with him shortly after he is released from hospital.

MARGUERITE

Marguerite is the only woman in the "gueules cassées". Having cut all ties with her rich family – who were all "either shirkers or rejected as unfit" – she signs up as a nurse at the front, where she is hit by a shell. However, the fact that her injury is so serious speaks volumes about how beautiful she must have been in the past. The three men praise her courage and kindness. The novel's other major female character is sanctified as a great icon of the war and inspires respect.

ANALYSIS

While most representations of war in literature tend towards lyricism, exalting the patriotism and courage of soldiers, Dugain immediately takes another approach, completely devoid of pomposity. His writing is simple and the language used in the novel is everyday, and even familiar at times.

A shortened war

"I knew nothing of the Great War." The first sentence we read in the novel seems rather paradoxical, and immediately differentiates the story from traditional war novels, which normally focus on the front and the trenches.

The First World War, as a succession of military and political events, is rarely brought up in the book: it is not spoken about much in the officers' ward. There are a few dates placed here and there throughout the novel, to give the reader some chronological reference points, but the events which go along with them are not always described. For example, the great Battle of Verdun in 1916 is not mentioned: the only battle plan in the book is the one the narrator's grandfather makes when preparing to gather mushrooms.

Time seems to stand still in the officers' ward. The only news for the injured soldiers is that of their daily suffering, not that of history: "The war was taking place far away, behind a curtain of smoke". Adrien has never seen his enemies' faces and only meets them after the armistice, at the signing of the Treaty of Versailles. He spends the four years of the war shut up in a hospital room, where he confronts his face, which he no longer recognises, and "the enemy within". The internal point of view adopted for the narration emphasises this tragic reflection.

An underlying antimilitarism

Adrien's lack of interest in the events which are going on outside, as well as the disgust and anger he feels about the growing number of casualties in the hospital, is sometimes mixed with bitter criticism of the army. The narrator's refusal to be seen as a hero (he declines the Legion of Honour at first) and to support the war is actually a subtle criticism of the men at the top who are orchestrating this bloody conflict. The Nivelle Offensive in 1917, for example, "the carnage that resulted was so great that for the first time, men with severe facial injuries had to be accommodated in the corridors". He also notes that they are always the only ones in the officers' ward, while the ordinary soldiers' ward is never empty. This implies that those higher up in the army tend not to take part in the actual fighting. In addition, the Minister of War's remark to Adrien (who has already paid a high price with his disfigured face) that he hopes he will soon be able to return to the front also appears ridiculous and misplaced. The same cynicism can also be seen from the head doctor, even though he is completely dedicated to his patients.

Indeed, he manages to take something positive from the war: seeing as the doctors have to try to repair the destroyed faces of the soldiers as best they can, maxillofacial surgery is forced to develop.

Wounded flesh

The many scenes which describe the combatants' trauma are marked with sobriety and realism. Dugain does not give the same morbid aesthetic depiction of the horrors of war as we are faced with in Louis-Ferdinand Céline's (French writer, 1894-1961) *Journey to the End of the Night* (1932).

The tragic episode of the attack on Adrien's regiment in Meuse, which is where he receives his terrible injury, is only described very briefly. It rounds off the second chapter in a masterful – and completely unexpected – way, and the narrator's use of the present reinforces the impression of instantaneity. As is often the case in the novel, the sentences are short – sometimes only made up of nouns – the rhythm is very rapid, and there is no link between prepositions: "I dismounted and settled down against a birch tree. There was a loud bang from somewhere close by. For a split second a whistling sound. [...] I feel like an axe has just been driven into the lower part of my nose. Then the lights go out".

The reader is subjected to the raw image of battered faces on almost every page. For example, when Penanster comes to the officers' ward, Adrien notes that "half his chin had been blown away by a shell which had also torn the carotid artery in passing. While Penenster lay on the ground after this first wound, a horse falling dead from an enemy bullet had kicked him in the face with its hoof". But there is never any sentimentality over the suffering we see in the novel:

the author includes this feeling only in the passages about love or nature. Suffering is present, but it is never developed. "The teeth had been pulverized [...] the pain in my sinuses returned and spread through all the tissues of my face", Adrien notes when he describes his own injuries in a brief, matter-of-fact manner. "And I couldn't say anything. Even if I could, I had nothing to say", he adds. The reader is never asked to show him pity.

The narrator adds mockery to certain descriptions, and sometimes even a macabre sense of humour, for example when he says his friend, a pilot who has sustained serious burns, has a "great toffee face", and the cavity of his lost eye to a "looted bird's nest". The author establishes a certain distance between the war and the injuries that it causes, and therefore never encourages any kind of pity.

THE ASSOCIATION OF THE WOUNDED TO THE FACE AND THE HEAD

According to the maxillofacial surgeon François-Xavier Long: "During the First World War, we saw more and people with facial injuries, which were not used to dealing with on such a large scale. During the conflict, 11 to 14% of casualties sustained injuries to the face. Of course, facial injuries have been around since Antiquity, but not to this extent. The rifles, shells, shrapnel and flamethrowers of the First World War caused considerable damage"[1] (Trouillard, *Grande Guerre : les Gueules cassées "faisaient tache dans la population"*, 2014).

During this period, between 10 000 and 15 000 men suffered facial injuries in France. Some of them were abandoned on the battlefield, left for dead even though they were still alive. The luckiest among them were taken from the front lines to the centres specialised in this kind of injury which begin to appear at this time. Val-de-Grâce, where Adrien is taken to, was one of them: the casualties benefitted from the considerable progress that had been made in reconstructive surgery.

After the war, disfigured soldiers were excluded from society. People would rather have forgotten this dark period of history, the traces of which were all too evident on these soldiers' faces. Moreover, they also had to deal with fleeting and unfriendly glances, sometimes even from their own families.

Although they were not recognised as war victims, these brothers-in-arms organised themselves and supported each other, which led to the foundation of the "Association of the Wounded to the Face and the Head" in 1921. Commonly known as the "gueules cassées" ("broken faces"), they decided to make their slogan as mocking as they could: "smile all the same".

This association was created by three men who were injured in the First World War: Colonel Picot (1862-1938), who came up with the expression "gueules cassées",

---

1. This quotation has been translated by BrightSummaries.com.

Bienaimé Jourdain (1890-1948) and Albert Jugon (1890-1959). Jugon was asked by the French President Georges Clémenceau to be one of the disfigured soldiers at the signing of the Treaty of Versailles on 28 June 1919. Dugain also makes his (fictional) protagonist a witness to this event in his novel.

From the battlefield to the officers' ward

The story sees Adrien go from the vast expanses of the Western Front to being shut up in a hospital room in the blink of an eye. The reader therefore moves away from the great collective history, taught in schoolbooks, to the individual story of Adrien, and from the mass carnage of the battlefields to the particular torture that the narrator endures on a daily basis, for example during the rehabilitation exercises in the "torture chamber".

The successive surgical operations which he goes through also illustrate this intrusive movement. They go through the skin of the face, exposing the inside of the skull and attacking the brain, the root of all thought, "digging deep into the tissue and nerve". The semantic fields used emphasise this idea of digging.

Besides their physical isolation in the hospital, the soldiers have to accept a certain withdrawal into themselves, a form of mental imprisonment, which limits their contact with the world around them.

Dehumanisation

Seeing as they often have ear, tongue or eye injuries, the soldiers have lost one or more of the senses which allowed them to communicate with others. Moreover, their faces, where we normally read expression, are unrecognisable. In order to convey this, Dugain often uses animal comparisons and metaphors, particularly with birds and their beaks (the soldiers' noses, a prominent feature of their faces, are often damaged). For example, the narrator comments that Penanster's rehabilitation will soon enable him to "open his mouth as wide as La Fontaine's crow its beak", compares himself to a white owl and regrets that Weil will have to make do with a nose that looks like "the top half of a bird's beak". Adrien also describes the "simian" faces in the room, and the skin grafts he describes often use animal cartilages.

The soldiers in the officers' ward are stripped of their ability to communicate, compared to birds or monkeys, reduced to making animal-like sounds and blended with beasts by the grafts. They therefore lose a part of their humanity.

Self-image

This frequent blending of the injured with animals cannot help but alter their self-image. Even if Adrien never mentions how he looked before, when Clémence found him attractive, he cannot help his involuntary, violent reaction when he sees the reflection of his ravaged face for the first time: "to my surprise, I felt no desire to cry, in fact I was not troubled at all. To my even greater surprise, my stomach heaved and I found myself emptying its entire contents over the borrowed bedcover", he comments.

Facial mutilation is the most damaging wound soldiers can suffer, because it affects their relationship that they have with themselves and with others far more than injuries to their lower body would. As a result, Penanster is chosen to make first contact with Marguerite because "his left profile was almost intact". Soldiers with facial injuries are therefore made to suffer not only physical injury, but also moral, narcissistic judgement.

THE FEMALE FIGURES

The novel's female figures are particularly important in this predominantly masculine world. There are three female images in the text, and each of them embodies a different feeling.

Clémence

Adrien is attracted to Clémence from the first time they meet, and he is certain that their brief relationship at the start of the novel will not be the last time they see each other. He thinks about the young woman throughout his stay at the hospital and tries to find her afterwards, even though she clearly rejected him and he knows that he is disfigured for life: "I knew I would see her again, even if it took months or years", the young man states. Clémence therefore represents love.

Marguerite

The first descriptions of Marguerite focus on what remains of her former beauty, and Adrien and his friends try to ingratiate themselves with her at first. However, they end up simply becoming friends. The soldiers admire her courage on the front and the way she stands up to adversity ("she told us her story. We listened in astonishment"). She represents courage.

The nurses and prostitutes

The nurses are in constant physical proximity with the injured officers, which encourages Adrien and his friends to flirt with them. They are delighted that the prettiest nurses are on their floor. However, they find out that this decision was made in order to put off anyone who might be thinking about getting involved with the patients. Nevertheless, Weil tries his luck with one of them, "working on the principle that charm had nothing to do with looks". However, he admits that he failed later on.

When it comes to prostitutes, the young officers have to pay a lot for their services because of their repulsive appearance. The officers' visit to them only confuses and embitters Adrien, who had never associated with them before the war.

The nurses and the prostitutes represent desire. Interacting with women is clearly the most difficult part of life now for these men who have lost their good looks.

A UNIQUE NOVEL

Unlike other novels, such as *14* by Jean Echenoz (French writer, born in 1947), *The Officers' Ward* only mentions the war indirectly. In *14*, the author describes the fate of five men at the outbreak of the First World War: the daily lives of these soldiers in the trenches is the focus of the story.

This is not the case in Dugain's novel, where the protagonist actually spends no more than a few days on the front lines before he is maimed by a shell and sent to hospital to be treated as best he can. The rest of the novel then takes place in Val-de-Grâce, well behind the front line, where the only soldiers he now interacts with are those who have also been injured. In doing this, the author takes a very original look at war.

After all, war literature focuses on trench life and what is involved more than anything else: days made up of waiting, mud and death, as is the case in *Under Fire* by Henri Barbusse (French writer, 1873-1935). Having been a soldier himself, Barbusse is keen to depict the true horror of war, describing all the atrocities that it entails. This is the case for other witnesses of this time, who give a soldier's point of view of daily life during the war. Besides these examples, we also find a whole range of fictional literature, sometimes written by authors who fought in the war. This is the case of Céline, who paints a biting picture of the war in the first part of *Journey to the End of the Night*. This antimilitarist novel highlights the sense of horror felt by every soldier and the absurdity of all this butchery:

"As for the colonel, I didn't wish him any hard luck. But he was dead too. At first I didn't see him The blast had carried him up the embankment and laid him down on his side, right in the arms of the dismounted cavalryman, the courier, who was finished too. They were embracing each other for the moment and for all eternity, but the cavalryman's head was gone, all he had was an opening at the top of the neck, with blood in it bubbling and glugging like jam in a kettle. The colonel's belly was wide open, and he was making a nasty face about it. [...] Tough shit for him! If he'd beat it when the shooting started, it wouldn't have happened" (p. 12).

In contrast to this description of the hell that soldiers in the trenches experience, Dugain presents a detailed analysis not of life on the front, but of the injuries of the disfigured. In this way, when the hospital doctor is examining an injured man, he describes the terrible facial injuries a shell has inflicted upon the unfortunate soldier with horrific detail. The lower half of his face is completely destroyed: there is little left of his upper jaw or his palate, and his tongue is in shreds.

The Officers' Ward therefore forces the reader to confront a reality which is often forgotten and very rarely mentioned. Throughout the novel, Dugain highlights the suffering inherent to war but, unlike Céline and other authors of war books, who show the violence of conflict, Dugain prefers to present a psychological portrait of the injured, and concentrates on an aspect which is not often brought up: how difficult it is for the "gueules cassées" to live and reintegrate into society after what has happened to them.

> "I knew nothing of the Great War. I knew nothing of the muddy trenches, the dampness that seeps into the bones, the big black rats in their winter fur dodging among the mounds of refuse, the stench – a mixture of cheap tobacco and half-buried excrement – and over everything, the unvaried metal-grey sky that unleashes a torrent of rain at regular intervals, as if God can never refrain from hounding the ordinary soldier.
> Of that war, I knew nothing."

Consequently, life in the trenches and on the front is not the only kind of war; there is also the war that the many casualties fight far behind the front lines.

FURTHER REFLECTION

SOME QUESTIONS TO THINK ABOUT...

- In what way does the classic structure of the novel convey the protagonist's state of mind?
- What are the similarities and differences between *The Officers' Ward* and the first part of Céline's *Journey to the End of the Night*?
- In what way can Adrien Fournier be considered an anti-hero?
- In what way do the soldiers' injuries contribute to their dehumanisation?
- "We had spoken to each other in a language of strange facial movements, like fish". In your opinion, why does communication occupy a central place in *The Officers' Ward*?
- Study the opposition between the city and the country-side, a recurring theme in the novel.
- The narrator references the myth of Sisyphus. In what way does this Greek myth illustrate his situation?
- Do you think the film adaptation of the novel is faithful to the source material? Justify your response with arguments and examples.
- Study Adrien's relationship with his family. In what way does it change after he is injured?
- Compare how the theme of war is treated in *The Officers' Ward*, and in *The Great Swindle* by Pierre Lemaitre (French writer and scriptwriter, born in 1951) and *14* (2012) by Jean Echenoz.

We want to hear from you!
Leave a comment on your online library
and share your favourite books on social media!

FURTHER READING

REFERENCE EDITION

- Dugain, M. (2001) *The Officers' Ward*. Trans. Curtis, H. London: Phoenix.

REFERENCE STUDIES

- Céline, L. F. (2006) *Journey to the End of the Night*. Trans. Manheim, R. New York: New Directions.
- Daley, P. (2014) Broken gargoyles: the disfigured soldiers of the first world war. *The Guardian*. [Online]. [Accessed 26 April 2017]. Available from: <https://www.theguardian.com/world/postcolonial/2014/may/26/broken-gargoyles-the-disfigured-soldiers-of-the-first-world-war>
- Kaiser, D. (No date) Treaty of Versailles. *History*. [Online]. [Accessed 26 April 2017]. Available from: <http://www.history.com/topics/world-war-i/treaty-of-versailles>
- Mosley, M. (No date) How do you fix a face that's been blown off by shrapnel? *BBC*. [Online]. [Accessed 26 April 2017]. Available from: <http://www.bbc.co.uk/guides/zxw42hv>

ADAPTATION

- *The Officers' Ward*. (2001) [Film]. François Dupeyron, dir. France: ARP Sélection.

www.brightsummaries.com

Ebook EAN: 9782806297327

Paperback EAN: 9782806297334

Legal Deposit: D/2017/12603/264

This guide was written with the collaboration of Alexandre Randal for the chapter 'A unique novel' and the section 'The Association of the wounded to the face and the head'.

Cover: © Primento

Digital conception by Primento, the digital partner of publishers.

This guide was produced with the support of the *Service Général des Lettres et du Livre* of the Wallonia-Brussels Federation.